50 Taste of Korea Dishes

By: Kelly Johnson

Table of Contents

- Kimchi
- Bibimbap
- Bulgogi
- Samgyeopsal
- Japchae
- Tteokbokki
- Kimchi Jjigae
- Banchan
- Galbi
- Jajangmyeon
- Sundubu Jjigae
- Kimbap
- Mandu
- Budae Jjigae
- Naengmyeon
- Kimchi Jeon
- Haejang-guk
- Doenjang Jjigae
- Gimbap
- Dakgalbi
- Sannakji
- Miyeok Guk
- Jjajangbap
- Yangnyeom Chicken
- Pajeon
- Ojingeo Bokkeum
- Gamjatang
- Gyeranjjim
- Banchan
- Hoe (Korean Raw Fish)
- Porridge (Juk)
- Cheonggukjang
- Hotteok
- Chimaek
- Ddukbokki

- Kimchi Bokkeumbap
- Yukhwe
- Banchan
- Cheonggukjang
- Galbitang
- Gochujang Jjigae
- Haepari
- Dolsot Bibimbap
- Tofu Jjigae
- Gochujang Grilled Pork
- Jeonbokjuk
- Oi Muchim
- Chamchi Kimchi Jjigae
- Gyeongju Bread
- Jangjorim

Kimchi

Ingredients:

- 1 medium napa cabbage
- 1/4 cup sea salt
- 2 cups water
- 1 tablespoon grated ginger
- 1 tablespoon garlic (minced)
- 2 tablespoons fish sauce
- 2 tablespoons sugar
- 1 tablespoon gochugaru (Korean chili flakes)
- 2 tablespoons gochujang (Korean chili paste)

Instructions:

1. **Prepare Cabbage:** Cut the napa cabbage into quarters and remove the core. Chop into bite-sized pieces and sprinkle with sea salt. Let sit for 2 hours to wilt.
2. **Make Paste:** Mix ginger, garlic, fish sauce, sugar, gochugaru, and gochujang in a bowl to form a paste.
3. **Mix:** Rinse cabbage thoroughly to remove excess salt. Massage the chili paste into the cabbage and pack it tightly into a jar.
4. **Ferment:** Leave at room temperature for 1-3 days, then store in the refrigerator.

Bibimbap

Ingredients:

- 1 cup cooked rice
- 1/2 cup spinach (blanched)
- 1/2 cup bean sprouts (blanched)
- 1/4 cup shredded carrots
- 1/4 cup shiitake mushrooms (sautéed)
- 1 egg (fried sunny-side-up)
- 2 tablespoons gochujang
- 1 tablespoon sesame oil
- 1 tablespoon sesame seeds

Instructions:

1. **Prepare Vegetables:** Blanch spinach and bean sprouts, sauté mushrooms, and julienne carrots.
2. **Assemble:** In a bowl, layer the cooked rice, vegetables, and fried egg on top.
3. **Serve:** Drizzle with sesame oil, gochujang, and sprinkle sesame seeds on top. Mix together before eating.

Bulgogi

Ingredients:

- 1 lb beef (thinly sliced, ribeye or sirloin)
- 1/4 cup soy sauce
- 2 tablespoons brown sugar
- 2 tablespoons sesame oil
- 2 tablespoons minced garlic
- 1 tablespoon grated ginger
- 1/2 medium onion (sliced)
- 1 tablespoon sesame seeds
- 1 tablespoon chopped green onions

Instructions:

1. **Marinate Beef:** Mix soy sauce, sugar, sesame oil, garlic, ginger, and onion in a bowl. Add the beef and marinate for at least 30 minutes.
2. **Cook:** Heat a pan or grill over medium-high heat. Cook marinated beef for 3-4 minutes until browned and tender.
3. **Serve:** Garnish with sesame seeds and green onions. Serve with rice or in lettuce wraps.

Samgyeopsal

Ingredients:

- 1 lb pork belly (sliced into thick strips)
- 2 tablespoons sesame oil
- 2 tablespoons gochujang
- 2 teaspoons garlic (minced)
- 1 tablespoon soy sauce
- Lettuce leaves (for wrapping)
- Sliced garlic, green onions, and kimchi (for serving)

Instructions:

1. **Grill Pork Belly:** Heat a grill pan over medium-high heat. Grill the pork belly strips until crispy and cooked through, about 3-4 minutes per side.
2. **Serve:** Serve the grilled pork with sesame oil, gochujang, and minced garlic on the side. Wrap the meat in lettuce leaves with garlic, green onions, and kimchi.

Japchae

Ingredients:

- 8 oz sweet potato noodles (dangmyeon)
- 1/2 lb beef (sliced thin)
- 1/2 onion (sliced)
- 1/2 carrot (julienned)
- 1/2 bell pepper (sliced)
- 2 tablespoons soy sauce
- 1 tablespoon sesame oil
- 1 tablespoon sugar
- 1 tablespoon sesame seeds

Instructions:

1. **Cook Noodles:** Boil the sweet potato noodles in water until tender (about 6-7 minutes). Drain and set aside.
2. **Cook Beef:** Stir-fry beef with a bit of sesame oil and soy sauce until browned.
3. **Stir-fry Vegetables:** Stir-fry onion, carrot, and bell pepper in sesame oil until tender.
4. **Combine:** Add cooked noodles, beef, and vegetables to a pan. Stir in sugar, soy sauce, and sesame oil. Toss everything together.
5. **Serve:** Garnish with sesame seeds and serve.

Tteokbokki

Ingredients:

- 1 lb chewy rice cakes (tteok)
- 1/4 cup gochujang
- 1 tablespoon sugar
- 2 tablespoons soy sauce
- 2 cups fish stock or water
- 1 boiled egg (optional)
- Green onions (for garnish)

Instructions:

1. **Prepare Rice Cakes:** Soak rice cakes in warm water for 30 minutes if they're dried.
2. **Make Sauce:** In a pan, combine gochujang, soy sauce, sugar, and fish stock. Bring to a simmer.
3. **Cook:** Add rice cakes to the pan and cook for 10-15 minutes until tender and coated in the sauce.
4. **Serve:** Top with boiled egg and green onions, then serve hot.

Kimchi Jjigae

Ingredients:

- 2 cups kimchi (chopped)
- 1/2 lb pork belly (sliced thin)
- 1 tablespoon gochujang
- 2 tablespoons soy sauce
- 1 tablespoon sesame oil
- 1/2 onion (sliced)
- 2 cups water or broth
- Tofu (optional)

Instructions:

1. **Cook Pork:** In a pot, heat sesame oil and sauté pork belly until browned.
2. **Add Kimchi:** Add kimchi and sauté for 5 minutes.
3. **Simmer:** Add soy sauce, gochujang, and water. Bring to a boil, then simmer for 20 minutes.
4. **Add Tofu:** If using tofu, add it in the last 10 minutes of cooking.
5. **Serve:** Serve hot with steamed rice.

Banchan

Ingredients:

- 1/2 cup kimchi
- 1/2 cup spinach (blanched)
- 1/2 cup bean sprouts (blanched)
- 1/2 cup pickled radish
- 1/2 cup sautéed mushrooms

Instructions:

1. **Prepare Sides:** Prepare various small side dishes like kimchi, spinach, and bean sprouts.
2. **Serve:** Arrange each side dish in small bowls to serve with rice and main dishes like bulgogi or bibimbap.

Galbi

Ingredients:

- 1 lb beef short ribs
- 1/4 cup soy sauce
- 2 tablespoons sesame oil
- 1 tablespoon garlic (minced)
- 1 tablespoon grated ginger
- 1/4 cup sugar
- 2 tablespoons rice vinegar

Instructions:

1. **Marinate Ribs:** Mix soy sauce, sesame oil, garlic, ginger, sugar, and rice vinegar in a bowl. Marinate the ribs for at least 2 hours.
2. **Grill:** Preheat the grill. Grill the marinated ribs over medium-high heat for 4-5 minutes per side until browned and cooked through.
3. **Serve:** Serve with steamed rice and vegetables.

Jajangmyeon

Ingredients:

- 8 oz fresh noodles (or dry, cooked)
- 1/2 lb pork (ground or sliced thin)
- 1/2 onion (diced)
- 1/2 zucchini (diced)
- 1/2 cup cabbage (shredded)
- 1 tablespoon garlic (minced)
- 3 tablespoons gochujang (Korean chili paste)
- 3 tablespoons black bean paste (chunjang)
- 2 tablespoons soy sauce
- 1 tablespoon sugar
- 2 cups water
- 1 tablespoon cornstarch (optional, to thicken)

Instructions:

1. **Cook Noodles:** Cook the noodles according to the package instructions, drain, and set aside.
2. **Stir-Fry Vegetables and Meat:** In a pan, sauté the pork until browned. Add onions, zucchini, cabbage, and garlic, and stir-fry until softened.
3. **Make Sauce:** Add gochujang, black bean paste, soy sauce, and sugar. Stir in water and bring to a simmer.
4. **Thicken:** Mix cornstarch with a little water and add it to the pan, stirring until the sauce thickens.
5. **Serve:** Toss the cooked noodles with the sauce and serve hot.

Sundubu Jjigae

Ingredients:

- 1/2 lb soft tofu (sundubu)
- 1/4 lb ground pork or beef
- 1 tablespoon gochujang (Korean chili paste)
- 1 tablespoon gochugaru (Korean chili flakes)
- 2 tablespoons sesame oil
- 2 tablespoons garlic (minced)
- 1/2 onion (sliced)
- 2 cups broth (beef or vegetable)
- 1 egg (optional)
- 2 green onions (sliced)

Instructions:

1. **Cook Meat:** Heat sesame oil in a pot. Add ground pork or beef and cook until browned.
2. **Add Vegetables:** Stir in garlic and onions, sauté until fragrant.
3. **Make Soup Base:** Add gochujang, gochugaru, and broth. Bring to a boil and simmer for 10 minutes.
4. **Add Tofu:** Gently add soft tofu to the pot. Let it simmer for another 5 minutes.
5. **Serve:** Crack an egg into the soup (optional) and cook until set. Garnish with green onions and serve hot with rice.

Kimbap

Ingredients:

- 2 cups cooked rice (short-grain, cooled)
- 10 sheets nori (seaweed)
- 1 cucumber (julienned)
- 2 eggs (scrambled)
- 1/2 lb cooked beef or fish cakes (optional)
- 1/4 cup pickled radish (sliced)
- 1 tablespoon sesame oil
- 1 tablespoon sesame seeds
- Soy sauce (for dipping)

Instructions:

1. **Prepare Fillings:** Prepare all fillings by cutting cucumber, scrambled eggs, and pickled radish into strips.
2. **Make Rice:** Mix cooled rice with sesame oil and sesame seeds.
3. **Assemble:** Place a sheet of nori on a bamboo mat. Spread a thin layer of rice, leaving a border at the top. Add fillings in a line along the bottom.
4. **Roll:** Roll the kimbap tightly, sealing with the border.
5. **Serve:** Slice the roll into bite-sized pieces and serve with soy sauce.

Mandu

Ingredients:

- 1/2 lb ground pork (or beef)
- 1/4 cup cabbage (shredded)
- 2 tablespoons garlic (minced)
- 1/4 onion (finely chopped)
- 1 tablespoon soy sauce
- 1 tablespoon sesame oil
- 1 tablespoon gochujang (optional)
- 1 pack mandu wrappers (store-bought or homemade)
- Water (for sealing wrappers)

Instructions:

1. **Make Filling:** In a bowl, combine ground meat, cabbage, garlic, onion, soy sauce, sesame oil, and gochujang (if using).
2. **Fill Wrappers:** Place a small spoonful of the filling in the center of each wrapper. Wet the edges with water and fold to seal.
3. **Cook Mandu:** You can steam, pan-fry, or boil the mandu. To pan-fry, heat oil in a pan and fry until golden on both sides.
4. **Serve:** Serve with dipping sauce made of soy sauce, sesame oil, and vinegar.

Budae Jjigae

Ingredients:

- 1/2 lb spam (or any canned meat)
- 1/2 lb hot dog sausage
- 1/2 lb tofu (cubed)
- 1 onion (sliced)
- 2 cups broth (beef or vegetable)
- 2 tablespoons gochujang
- 1 tablespoon soy sauce
- 2 cups kimchi
- 2 green onions (sliced)
- 1 package ramen noodles

Instructions:

1. **Prepare Ingredients:** Slice the spam, sausages, tofu, and onion.
2. **Simmer Soup:** In a pot, combine all ingredients (except ramen) and simmer for 15 minutes, stirring occasionally.
3. **Add Ramen:** Add ramen noodles and cook until soft.
4. **Serve:** Garnish with green onions and serve hot.

Naengmyeon

Ingredients:

- 8 oz naengmyeon noodles (buckwheat or sweet potato starch noodles)
- 1/2 cucumber (julienned)
- 1 boiled egg (sliced)
- 1/2 pear (sliced thin)
- 1 tablespoon gochujang (optional)
- 1 tablespoon vinegar
- 2 tablespoons soy sauce
- 1 tablespoon sugar
- 2 cups cold beef broth

Instructions:

1. **Cook Noodles:** Boil the naengmyeon noodles according to package instructions. Drain and rinse under cold water.
2. **Prepare Broth:** In a bowl, mix beef broth, vinegar, soy sauce, sugar, and gochujang.
3. **Assemble:** Place noodles in a bowl, add cold broth, and top with cucumber, pear, and boiled egg.
4. **Serve:** Serve immediately with optional side of kimchi.

Kimchi Jeon

Ingredients:

- 1 cup kimchi (chopped)
- 1/2 cup flour
- 1/2 cup water
- 1 egg (beaten)
- 1 tablespoon sesame oil
- 1 tablespoon soy sauce
- 1/4 onion (sliced)

Instructions:

1. **Make Batter:** In a bowl, mix flour, water, and egg to create a batter. Stir in chopped kimchi and onion.
2. **Fry Pancakes:** Heat sesame oil in a pan over medium heat. Pour in a portion of the batter and flatten it into a pancake shape. Fry until crispy on both sides.
3. **Serve:** Serve hot with soy sauce for dipping.

Haejang-guk

Ingredients:

- 1/2 lb beef short ribs (or brisket)
- 1/2 onion (sliced)
- 2 tablespoons gochujang
- 1 tablespoon soy sauce
- 1 tablespoon garlic (minced)
- 2 cups broth (beef or vegetable)
- 2 cups kimchi
- 1 tablespoon sesame oil
- Green onions (for garnish)

Instructions:

1. **Cook Meat:** In a pot, brown beef short ribs with sesame oil. Add onion and garlic and sauté.
2. **Add Broth:** Add broth, gochujang, soy sauce, and kimchi. Bring to a boil, then simmer for 1-2 hours until the beef is tender.
3. **Serve:** Garnish with green onions and serve hot.

Doenjang Jjigae

Ingredients:

- 1/2 cup doenjang (fermented soybean paste)
- 1/2 lb tofu (cubed)
- 1/2 onion (sliced)
- 2 cups broth (vegetable or beef)
- 1/2 zucchini (sliced)
- 1 tablespoon gochujang (optional)
- 2 green onions (sliced)

Instructions:

1. **Prepare Soup Base:** In a pot, dissolve doenjang in broth, bringing it to a boil.
2. **Add Vegetables and Tofu:** Add zucchini, onion, and tofu. Simmer for 10-15 minutes.
3. **Season:** Stir in gochujang for extra spice.
4. **Serve:** Garnish with green onions and serve with rice.

Gimbap (Korean Sushi Roll)

Ingredients:

- 2 cups cooked rice (short-grain, cooled)
- 10 sheets nori (seaweed)
- 1 cucumber (julienned)
- 2 eggs (scrambled)
- 1/4 lb cooked beef (or fish cakes)
- 1/4 cup pickled radish (sliced)
- 1 tablespoon sesame oil
- 1 tablespoon sesame seeds
- Soy sauce (for dipping)

Instructions:

1. **Prepare Rice:** Mix the cooled rice with sesame oil and sesame seeds.
2. **Prepare Fillings:** Slice cucumber, scramble the eggs, and prepare the pickled radish.
3. **Assemble Gimbap:** Place a sheet of nori on a bamboo mat. Spread a thin layer of rice, leaving a border at the top. Add the fillings in a line along the bottom.
4. **Roll:** Roll tightly, sealing the edge with water.
5. **Serve:** Slice the roll into bite-sized pieces and serve with soy sauce for dipping.

Dakgalbi (Spicy Stir-Fried Chicken)

Ingredients:

- 1 lb chicken thighs (boneless, cut into bite-sized pieces)
- 1 tablespoon sesame oil
- 2 tablespoons gochujang (Korean chili paste)
- 1 tablespoon soy sauce
- 1 tablespoon garlic (minced)
- 1 tablespoon ginger (minced)
- 2 tablespoons honey
- 1/2 onion (sliced)
- 1 carrot (sliced)
- 2 cups cabbage (shredded)
- 2 tablespoons gochugaru (chili flakes)

Instructions:

1. **Prepare Marinade:** In a bowl, mix gochujang, soy sauce, garlic, ginger, honey, and gochugaru.
2. **Marinate Chicken:** Add the chicken to the marinade, mix well, and refrigerate for at least 30 minutes.
3. **Stir-Fry:** Heat sesame oil in a pan. Add the chicken and stir-fry until browned.
4. **Add Vegetables:** Add onion, carrot, and cabbage. Stir-fry for another 5-10 minutes until vegetables are tender.
5. **Serve:** Serve hot with steamed rice.

Sannakji (Live Octopus)

Ingredients:

- 1 live octopus (sannakji)
- Sesame oil
- Sesame seeds
- Salt

Instructions:

1. **Prepare Octopus:** Clean and cut the live octopus into small, bite-sized pieces.
2. **Serve:** Drizzle with sesame oil, sprinkle sesame seeds, and salt. Serve immediately while the tentacles are still moving.

Miyeok Guk (Seaweed Soup)

Ingredients:

- 1/2 cup dried miyeok (seaweed)
- 5 oz beef (or anchovies for broth)
- 6 cups water
- 2 tablespoons soy sauce
- 1 tablespoon sesame oil
- 1 clove garlic (minced)

Instructions:

1. **Soak Seaweed:** Soak the miyeok in water for 20-30 minutes. Drain and cut into bite-sized pieces.
2. **Make Broth:** In a pot, bring water to a boil with beef or anchovies for the broth.
3. **Cook Seaweed:** Add the soaked seaweed, soy sauce, sesame oil, and garlic. Simmer for 30 minutes.
4. **Serve:** Serve hot, traditionally with rice and kimchi.

Jjajangbap (Rice with Black Bean Paste Sauce)

Ingredients:

- 1 cup cooked rice
- 1/2 lb pork (ground)
- 1/2 onion (chopped)
- 1/4 zucchini (chopped)
- 2 tablespoons chunjang (black bean paste)
- 1 tablespoon gochujang (Korean chili paste)
- 2 tablespoons soy sauce
- 1 tablespoon sugar
- 1 cup water

Instructions:

1. **Cook Pork:** Brown the ground pork in a pan.
2. **Add Vegetables:** Add onion and zucchini, cooking until softened.
3. **Make Sauce:** Stir in chunjang, gochujang, soy sauce, and sugar. Add water and simmer for 10-15 minutes.
4. **Serve:** Spoon the sauce over hot rice and serve.

Yangnyeom Chicken (Korean Fried Chicken)

Ingredients:

- 1 lb chicken wings (or drumsticks)
- 1/4 cup cornstarch
- 1/4 cup flour
- 1 egg
- 2 cups oil (for frying)

For Sauce:

- 2 tablespoons gochujang
- 2 tablespoons soy sauce
- 1 tablespoon honey
- 1 tablespoon garlic (minced)
- 1 tablespoon vinegar
- 1 tablespoon sesame oil

Instructions:

1. **Prepare Chicken:** Coat chicken in cornstarch, flour, and egg.
2. **Fry Chicken:** Heat oil in a pan and fry chicken until golden and crispy.
3. **Make Sauce:** Combine gochujang, soy sauce, honey, garlic, vinegar, and sesame oil.
4. **Coat Chicken:** Toss fried chicken in the sauce and serve immediately.

Pajeon (Korean Green Onion Pancake)

Ingredients:

- 1 cup flour
- 1/2 cup water
- 1 egg
- 2 cups green onions (cut into 2-inch pieces)
- 1/2 cup seafood (optional, shrimp or squid)
- 1 tablespoon sesame oil
- Soy sauce (for dipping)

Instructions:

1. **Make Batter:** Mix flour, water, and egg into a batter.
2. **Add Fillings:** Stir in green onions and seafood.
3. **Fry Pancakes:** Heat sesame oil in a pan and pour in the batter to form a pancake. Cook until golden on both sides.
4. **Serve:** Cut into slices and serve with soy sauce for dipping.

Ojingeo Bokkeum (Spicy Stir-Fried Squid)

Ingredients:

- 2 squid (cleaned and sliced)
- 2 tablespoons gochujang
- 1 tablespoon gochugaru (chili flakes)
- 1 tablespoon soy sauce
- 1 tablespoon sesame oil
- 1/2 onion (sliced)
- 1 bell pepper (sliced)
- 2 tablespoons garlic (minced)

Instructions:

1. **Cook Squid:** Heat sesame oil in a pan. Add squid and cook for 2-3 minutes until tender.
2. **Stir-Fry Vegetables:** Add onion, bell pepper, and garlic. Stir-fry for a few minutes.
3. **Make Sauce:** Add gochujang, gochugaru, and soy sauce. Stir to coat.
4. **Serve:** Serve hot with rice.

Gamjatang (Spicy Pork Bone Soup)

Ingredients:

- 1 lb pork neck bones
- 6 cups water
- 2 tablespoons gochujang
- 1 tablespoon sesame oil
- 1 tablespoon garlic (minced)
- 2 tablespoons soybean paste (doenjang)
- 1 potato (peeled and cubed)
- 2 cups napa cabbage (cut)
- 2 green onions (sliced)

Instructions:

1. **Boil Pork:** Boil pork neck bones for 1-2 hours to make a rich broth.
2. **Add Vegetables:** Add gochujang, sesame oil, garlic, soybean paste, potato, and napa cabbage.
3. **Simmer:** Simmer for 30 minutes until potatoes are tender.
4. **Serve:** Garnish with green onions and serve hot.

Gyeranjjim (Korean Steamed Egg)

Ingredients:

- 4 eggs
- 1 cup water or broth
- 1 tablespoon soy sauce
- 1/2 teaspoon sesame oil
- 1/4 teaspoon salt
- Green onions (for garnish)

Instructions:

1. **Prepare Eggs:** Beat eggs in a bowl. Add water or broth, soy sauce, sesame oil, and salt.
2. **Steam Eggs:** Pour egg mixture into a heatproof bowl and steam over low heat for 10-15 minutes, stirring halfway.
3. **Serve:** Garnish with sliced green onions and serve hot.

Banchan (Korean Side Dishes)

Ingredients (for various Banchan):

- Kimchi (fermented vegetables, usually napa cabbage or radish)
- Bokkeumbap (fried rice)
- Spinach (seasoned with sesame oil and garlic)
- Pickled vegetables (like radishes or cucumbers)
- Sautéed mushrooms
- Tofu (fried or steamed with soy sauce and sesame oil)
- Bean sprouts (seasoned with garlic and sesame oil)

Instructions:

1. **Prepare Banchan:** Each Banchan dish is usually made separately with simple seasoning, often featuring a mix of fermented, pickled, or sautéed ingredients.
2. **Serve:** Place multiple Banchan in small dishes and serve alongside rice and main dishes.

Hoe (Korean Raw Fish)

Ingredients:

- 1 lb fresh fish (often tuna, flounder, or other sushi-grade fish)
- 1 tablespoon gochujang (Korean chili paste)
- 1 tablespoon sesame oil
- 1 tablespoon soy sauce
- 1/2 tablespoon garlic (minced)
- 1 tablespoon rice vinegar
- Fresh vegetables (cucumber, radish, and lettuce for wrapping)
- Sesame seeds

Instructions:

1. **Prepare Fish:** Slice the fish thinly and arrange it on a plate.
2. **Make Sauce:** Mix gochujang, soy sauce, sesame oil, garlic, and rice vinegar.
3. **Serve:** Drizzle the sauce over the fish. Garnish with sesame seeds and serve with fresh vegetables like cucumber, radish, and lettuce for wrapping.

Porridge (Juk)

Ingredients:

- 1 cup rice
- 5 cups water (or chicken/vegetable broth)
- 1/2 cup chicken breast or beef (optional, shredded)
- 1 tablespoon sesame oil
- Salt to taste
- 1/4 cup green onions (chopped)
- 1 tablespoon soy sauce (optional)

Instructions:

1. **Cook Rice:** Wash rice and add it to a pot with water or broth. Bring to a boil and then simmer over low heat for 40-50 minutes, stirring occasionally.
2. **Add Protein:** If using chicken or beef, add shredded meat to the pot in the final 10 minutes of cooking.
3. **Season:** Stir in sesame oil, soy sauce, and salt.
4. **Serve:** Top with green onions and serve hot.

Cheonggukjang (Fermented Soybean Stew)

Ingredients:

- 1/2 cup cheonggukjang (fermented soybean paste)
- 6 cups water or broth
- 1/2 onion (chopped)
- 1/2 zucchini (sliced)
- 1/2 cup tofu (cut into cubes)
- 2 tablespoons garlic (minced)
- 1 tablespoon sesame oil
- Salt and pepper to taste

Instructions:

1. **Prepare Broth:** Bring water or broth to a boil and add cheonggukjang. Stir to dissolve the paste.
2. **Add Vegetables:** Add onion, zucchini, garlic, and tofu to the pot.
3. **Simmer:** Let the stew simmer for 10-15 minutes.
4. **Season:** Stir in sesame oil, salt, and pepper. Serve hot.

Hotteok (Sweet Korean Pancakes)

Ingredients:

- 2 cups flour
- 1 tablespoon sugar
- 1/2 teaspoon salt
- 1 tablespoon yeast
- 1/2 cup warm water
- 1 tablespoon vegetable oil
- 1/2 cup brown sugar
- 1/2 cup chopped walnuts or peanuts
- 1 teaspoon cinnamon

Instructions:

1. **Prepare Dough:** Mix flour, sugar, salt, yeast, and warm water to form a dough. Let it rise for 1 hour.
2. **Make Filling:** Mix brown sugar, walnuts or peanuts, and cinnamon to create the filling.
3. **Shape Pancakes:** Divide the dough into balls. Flatten each ball and place a spoonful of filling in the center, then seal and shape it into a pancake.
4. **Cook:** Heat oil in a pan and cook the pancakes, pressing them flat as they cook, until both sides are golden brown.
5. **Serve:** Serve hot as a sweet snack.

Chimaek (Korean Fried Chicken and Beer)

Ingredients:

- 1 lb chicken wings or drumsticks
- 1 cup flour
- 1/2 cup cornstarch
- 1 egg
- 1 cup cold water
- 2 tablespoons soy sauce
- 1 tablespoon gochujang
- 1 tablespoon honey
- 1 tablespoon sesame oil
- Cold beer (for drinking)

Instructions:

1. **Prepare Chicken:** Coat chicken pieces in a mixture of flour, cornstarch, and egg. Dip them into cold water before frying.
2. **Fry Chicken:** Heat oil in a pan and fry the chicken until golden brown and crispy.
3. **Make Sauce:** In a separate pan, mix soy sauce, gochujang, honey, and sesame oil. Stir-fry for 2-3 minutes.
4. **Coat Chicken:** Toss the fried chicken in the sauce and serve with cold beer.

Ddukbokki (Spicy Rice Cakes)

Ingredients:

- 1 lb rice cakes (tteok)
- 2 tablespoons gochujang
- 1 tablespoon soy sauce
- 1 tablespoon sugar
- 1 tablespoon sesame oil
- 2 tablespoons garlic (minced)
- 1/2 onion (sliced)
- 1 boiled egg (optional)
- Green onions (for garnish)

Instructions:

1. **Cook Rice Cakes:** Boil rice cakes in water for 5-7 minutes until soft.
2. **Prepare Sauce:** In a pan, combine gochujang, soy sauce, sugar, sesame oil, and garlic. Stir well.
3. **Stir-Fry:** Add the rice cakes and onions to the pan, stir to coat with the sauce, and cook for 5-7 minutes.
4. **Serve:** Top with a boiled egg and garnish with green onions. Serve hot.

Kimchi Bokkeumbap (Kimchi Fried Rice)

Ingredients:

- 2 cups cooked rice
- 1 cup kimchi (chopped)
- 2 tablespoons soy sauce
- 1 tablespoon sesame oil
- 1 tablespoon gochujang (optional)
- 2 eggs (scrambled)
- 1/4 cup green onions (chopped)
- 1 tablespoon sesame seeds

Instructions:

1. **Prepare Rice:** Heat sesame oil in a pan and add kimchi. Stir-fry for 2-3 minutes.
2. **Add Rice:** Add the rice and soy sauce, stir-frying for 5 minutes.
3. **Scramble Eggs:** Push rice to the side of the pan and scramble the eggs in the same pan.
4. **Serve:** Mix the scrambled eggs into the rice and garnish with green onions and sesame seeds.

Yukhwe (Korean Beef Tartare)

Ingredients:

- 1/2 lb fresh beef tenderloin (sliced thinly)
- 1 tablespoon soy sauce
- 1 teaspoon sesame oil
- 1 teaspoon sugar
- 1/4 teaspoon garlic (minced)
- 1 egg yolk
- 1 tablespoon sesame seeds
- Green onions (for garnish)

Instructions:

1. **Prepare Beef:** Slice the beef tenderloin thinly and arrange on a plate.
2. **Make Sauce:** Mix soy sauce, sesame oil, sugar, and garlic in a bowl.
3. **Serve:** Drizzle the sauce over the beef, top with the egg yolk, sesame seeds, and green onions. Serve immediately.

Banchan (Korean Side Dishes)

Ingredients (for various Banchan):

- **Kimchi** (fermented napa cabbage or radish)
- **Bokkeumbap** (fried rice with vegetables)
- **Spinach** (seasoned with sesame oil and garlic)
- **Pickled Vegetables** (cucumbers, radishes)
- **Sautéed Mushrooms**
- **Tofu** (fried or steamed with soy sauce and sesame oil)
- **Bean Sprouts** (seasoned with garlic and sesame oil)

Instructions:

1. **Prepare Banchan:** Make each Banchan dish separately, typically with ingredients like vegetables, fermented foods, and lightly cooked items.
2. **Serve:** Serve the Banchan in small dishes alongside rice and main courses.

Cheonggukjang (Fermented Soybean Stew)

Ingredients:

- 1/2 cup **cheonggukjang** (fermented soybean paste)
- 6 cups water or broth
- 1/2 onion (chopped)
- 1/2 zucchini (sliced)
- 1/2 cup tofu (cut into cubes)
- 2 tablespoons garlic (minced)
- 1 tablespoon sesame oil
- Salt and pepper to taste

Instructions:

1. **Prepare Broth:** Bring water or broth to a boil and add the cheonggukjang, stirring to dissolve it.
2. **Add Vegetables and Tofu:** Add onion, zucchini, garlic, and tofu to the pot.
3. **Simmer:** Let the stew simmer for about 15 minutes.
4. **Season:** Stir in sesame oil, salt, and pepper. Serve hot.

Galbitang (Beef Short Rib Soup)

Ingredients:

- 1 lb beef short ribs (cut into pieces)
- 10 cups water
- 3 garlic cloves (whole)
- 1 onion (halved)
- 1 tablespoon soy sauce
- 1 tablespoon sesame oil
- Salt and pepper to taste
- 1/4 cup green onions (chopped)
- Cooked rice (to serve)

Instructions:

1. **Prepare Ribs:** Blanch the short ribs in boiling water for 5 minutes to remove impurities, then drain.
2. **Cook Soup:** In a large pot, add the ribs, water, garlic, and onion. Bring to a boil, then reduce to a simmer for 1-2 hours until the ribs are tender.
3. **Season:** Add soy sauce, sesame oil, salt, and pepper. Continue simmering for another 10-15 minutes.
4. **Serve:** Remove the garlic and onion. Serve the soup with green onions and a bowl of rice.

Gochujang Jjigae (Spicy Red Pepper Paste Stew)

Ingredients:

- 1/2 lb pork or beef (cut into bite-sized pieces)
- 1 onion (sliced)
- 1 zucchini (sliced)
- 1/2 cup kimchi (chopped)
- 1 tablespoon gochujang (Korean chili paste)
- 1 tablespoon soy sauce
- 4 cups water or broth
- 2 tablespoons sesame oil
- 1 tablespoon garlic (minced)
- Salt and pepper to taste
- 1/4 cup green onions (chopped)

Instructions:

1. **Cook Meat:** Heat sesame oil in a pot, and cook the meat until browned.
2. **Add Vegetables:** Add onion, zucchini, and kimchi, and sauté for a few minutes.
3. **Make Stew:** Add gochujang, soy sauce, water (or broth), garlic, salt, and pepper. Bring to a boil, then simmer for 20 minutes.
4. **Serve:** Garnish with chopped green onions and serve hot.

Haepari (Korean Fish Soup)

Ingredients:

- 1 whole fish (preferably yellow corvina or snapper)
- 1 onion (quartered)
- 2 tablespoons gochugaru (Korean chili flakes)
- 2 tablespoons soy sauce
- 1 tablespoon sesame oil
- 4 cups water
- 2 tablespoons garlic (minced)
- 1 tablespoon ginger (minced)
- 1/4 cup green onions (chopped)
- Salt and pepper to taste

Instructions:

1. **Prepare Fish:** Clean and gut the fish, removing scales and internal organs.
2. **Make Broth:** In a large pot, add the fish, onion, garlic, ginger, and water. Bring to a boil and simmer for about 20 minutes.
3. **Add Seasoning:** Add gochugaru, soy sauce, sesame oil, salt, and pepper. Let simmer for an additional 10 minutes.
4. **Serve:** Remove the fish from the soup, discard bones, and serve the fish pieces with the broth. Garnish with green onions.

Dolsot Bibimbap (Hot Stone Pot Bibimbap)

Ingredients:

- 2 cups cooked rice
- 1/2 cup spinach (blanched)
- 1/2 cup bean sprouts (blanched)
- 1/2 carrot (julienned)
- 1/2 zucchini (julienned)
- 1 egg (fried sunny-side up)
- 2 tablespoons gochujang (Korean chili paste)
- 1 tablespoon sesame oil
- 1 tablespoon soy sauce
- 1 teaspoon garlic (minced)
- 1 tablespoon sesame seeds
- 1 tablespoon vegetable oil (for frying)

Instructions:

1. **Prepare Ingredients:** Blanch spinach and bean sprouts, sauté carrots and zucchini in sesame oil until tender.
2. **Assemble Bibimbap:** In a hot stone pot (or regular pot), add a layer of cooked rice. Arrange the spinach, bean sprouts, carrots, zucchini, and fried egg on top of the rice.
3. **Season:** Drizzle with sesame oil, soy sauce, and gochujang. Sprinkle with sesame seeds.
4. **Serve:** Mix everything together before eating to enjoy the flavors.

Tofu Jjigae (Tofu Stew)

Ingredients:

- 1 block soft tofu (cubed)
- 1 onion (sliced)
- 1 zucchini (sliced)
- 1/2 cup kimchi (chopped)
- 2 tablespoons gochujang (Korean chili paste)
- 4 cups water or vegetable broth
- 2 tablespoons sesame oil
- 2 tablespoons garlic (minced)
- Salt and pepper to taste
- 1/4 cup green onions (chopped)

Instructions:

1. **Sauté Vegetables:** Heat sesame oil in a pot. Add garlic and onions and sauté until fragrant.
2. **Add Kimchi and Gochujang:** Add the chopped kimchi and gochujang to the pot and stir well.
3. **Simmer:** Pour in the water or vegetable broth and bring to a boil. Reduce to a simmer for 10 minutes.
4. **Add Tofu:** Gently add the tofu cubes and zucchini to the stew. Simmer for an additional 5-10 minutes.
5. **Season:** Season with salt and pepper to taste.
6. **Serve:** Garnish with chopped green onions and serve hot.

Gochujang Grilled Pork (Gochujang Samgyeopsal)

Ingredients:

- 1 lb pork belly (sliced into thin strips)
- 2 tablespoons gochujang (Korean chili paste)
- 1 tablespoon soy sauce
- 1 tablespoon sesame oil
- 1 tablespoon garlic (minced)
- 1 tablespoon honey or sugar
- 1 tablespoon rice vinegar
- 1/2 teaspoon black pepper
- 1/4 cup sesame seeds (optional)

Instructions:

1. **Prepare Marinade:** In a bowl, mix gochujang, soy sauce, sesame oil, garlic, honey, rice vinegar, and black pepper.
2. **Marinate Pork:** Coat the pork belly slices in the marinade and let them sit for at least 30 minutes (or longer for better flavor).
3. **Grill:** Preheat the grill or grill pan. Grill the pork belly strips over medium heat until crispy and cooked through, about 4-5 minutes per side.
4. **Serve:** Garnish with sesame seeds, and serve with steamed rice and lettuce leaves for wrapping.

Jeonbokjuk (Abalone Porridge)

Ingredients:

- 2-3 abalones (fresh or canned)
- 1 cup short-grain rice
- 6 cups water or broth
- 2 tablespoons sesame oil
- 2 tablespoons garlic (minced)
- 1 tablespoon ginger (minced)
- 1 tablespoon soy sauce
- Salt to taste
- 1/4 cup green onions (chopped)

Instructions:

1. **Cook Rice:** Rinse the rice and add it to a pot with water or broth. Cook over medium heat until the rice is soft, about 20-25 minutes.
2. **Prepare Abalone:** If using fresh abalone, clean and slice it thinly.
3. **Make Porridge:** In a separate pan, heat sesame oil. Add garlic and ginger and sauté until fragrant. Add the abalone and cook for 2-3 minutes.
4. **Combine:** Add the cooked rice to the pan with the abalone and stir to combine. Add soy sauce and simmer for 10 minutes.
5. **Season:** Season with salt to taste.
6. **Serve:** Garnish with chopped green onions and serve hot.

Oi Muchim (Spicy Cucumber Salad)

Ingredients:

- 2 cucumbers (sliced thin)
- 2 tablespoons gochugaru (Korean chili flakes)
- 1 tablespoon sesame oil
- 1 tablespoon rice vinegar
- 1 tablespoon soy sauce
- 1 teaspoon sugar
- 1 tablespoon garlic (minced)
- 1 tablespoon sesame seeds
- 1/4 cup green onions (chopped)
- Salt to taste

Instructions:

1. **Prepare Cucumbers:** Slice the cucumbers and sprinkle with a pinch of salt. Let them sit for 10-15 minutes, then drain excess water.
2. **Make Dressing:** In a bowl, combine gochugaru, sesame oil, rice vinegar, soy sauce, sugar, and garlic.
3. **Toss Salad:** Add the cucumbers to the bowl and toss to coat with the dressing.
4. **Serve:** Garnish with sesame seeds and chopped green onions before serving.

Chamchi Kimchi Jjigae (Tuna Kimchi Stew)

Ingredients:

- 1 can tuna (drained)
- 1 cup kimchi (chopped)
- 1 onion (sliced)
- 1 tablespoon gochujang (Korean chili paste)
- 4 cups water or broth
- 2 tablespoons sesame oil
- 2 tablespoons garlic (minced)
- 1 tablespoon soy sauce
- Salt and pepper to taste
- 1/4 cup green onions (chopped)

Instructions:

1. **Prepare Soup Base:** Heat sesame oil in a pot. Add garlic, onion, and sauté until fragrant.
2. **Add Kimchi and Tuna:** Add the chopped kimchi and tuna to the pot and cook for 5 minutes.
3. **Add Broth:** Pour in water or broth and bring to a boil.
4. **Season:** Add gochujang, soy sauce, salt, and pepper. Let simmer for 10-15 minutes.
5. **Serve:** Garnish with chopped green onions and serve hot.

Gyeongju Bread (Hwangnam-ppang)

Ingredients:

- 2 cups all-purpose flour
- 1/2 cup warm water
- 1/4 cup sugar
- 2 tablespoons vegetable oil
- 1 teaspoon instant yeast
- 1/2 teaspoon salt
- 1/4 cup red bean paste (sweetened)
- 1 egg (beaten, for brushing)

Instructions:

1. **Prepare Dough:** In a bowl, combine warm water, sugar, and yeast. Let sit for 5 minutes to activate. Add flour, oil, and salt to form a dough. Knead for 10 minutes.
2. **Let Dough Rise:** Cover the dough and let it rise in a warm place for about 1 hour, or until it doubles in size.
3. **Form Bread:** Divide dough into small portions and roll each into a flat circle. Place a spoonful of red bean paste in the center and fold the dough to enclose the filling.
4. **Bake:** Place the filled dough on a baking sheet, brush with egg wash, and bake at 350°F (175°C) for 15-20 minutes until golden brown.
5. **Serve:** Let cool slightly before serving.

Jangjorim (Soy Braised Beef)

Ingredients:

- 1 lb beef brisket or shank (cut into strips)
- 2 tablespoons soy sauce
- 2 tablespoons sesame oil
- 1 tablespoon garlic (minced)
- 2 tablespoons brown sugar
- 1/4 cup water
- 1 tablespoon sesame seeds
- 2 green chilies (sliced)
- 1/4 cup green onions (chopped)

Instructions:

1. **Cook Beef:** In a pot, add beef, soy sauce, sesame oil, garlic, sugar, and water. Bring to a boil, then reduce to a simmer. Cook for 30-40 minutes until the beef is tender.
2. **Finish Cooking:** Add sesame seeds, green chilies, and green onions, then cook for an additional 5 minutes.
3. **Serve:** Serve the braised beef with steamed rice.

www.ingramcontent.com/pod-product-compliance
Lightning Source LLC
LaVergne TN
LVHW081505060526
838201LV00056BA/2941